NO SMALL
COMFORT

T0164163

NO SMALL COMFORT

Brian Simoneau

www.blacklawrence.com

Executive Editor: Diane Goettel
Cover Design: Zoe Norvell
Cover Art: "Winter 3.14" by Shawna Eberle
Book Design: Amy Freels

Published 2021 by Black Lawrence Press.
Printed in the United States.

for Tregony, Amelia, Harper, and Phoebe

Contents

******

Evidence of Having Been Here

A Lake Opens Up Beneath Your Feet

Like the sound you imagine a bone
makes as it breaks if you never broke
      a bone, atonal snap that's nothing
like rifle crack or thunder clap
      or knot in a crackling log. Like
a twig crunching underfoot only
      if you're standing only on twigs
over a deep hole you didn't know
      was waiting but are now certain is
studded with sharpened stakes, your breath
      gripped. There's no simile for such sound—no
metaphor for thuds, thumps, crashes, passing
      seconds contracting the space around
the brain—only the sound of the sound,
      every echo unsayable. Of course
if you're not alone, or if you're alone
      and getting it down in lines is what
crosses your mind, then you're not really
      hearing it right because it happens
so fast, so fucking fast, but perhaps
      it's beside the point since even
those who've never heard the silence of
      snow will know ice breaking
when it begins to break beneath them.

Landscape with Primary Colors

California hills gone gold, summer sky
blue enough to confuse, so clear, so sharp

the contrast. But there should always be three
you say, and here I've said only yellow

clipped by imponderable blue—you missed it
taking flight from a field of Spanish wheat

hackles streaked with blood: black sweep of raven
leaving behind a picked-over carcass;

raven who they say hunts with wolves and waits
beside battlefields for the fallen to die

who they say can forecast rain, who created
rivers and seas, who they say once sat

at the sides of gods, whose white was burned black
for stealing the sun and setting its light

in a sky like this; raven whose croaks and caws
when we're walking alone in the woods

remind us we are tethered to this earth
in ways that all of our gods are not.

The Morning Air Is All Awash with Angels

Today the neighbors' laundry
left on the line overnight
catches the last drops of rain.
A cup of tea is cooling
on the busy desk. Books lie

open, unfinished stanzas.
Somebody's already won
a car; the new Bob Barker
tells him spin again to win
a thousand bucks, a bonus

spin. Traffic on the bridge is
back to normal, be prepared
for minor delays along
the coast. The worst is over.
There's poker on two stations:

some are better than others
at waiting for luck to come
around. All I do some days
is wait for mail, wait for it
to be lunchtime. They say it's

love that calls us to the things
of this world. I find myself
hoping today that nothing
distracts from dust descending
in a single shaft of light.

Late Night, Walking Home

(Fourth of July)

The stoplight's steady red to green replaced
with blinking amber, tonight's sky empty

with ambient light, the road's deserted
where today you couldn't have counted

cars coursing along, coming together
and pulling apart like fallen leaves

squeezed between boulders in a storm-fed stream
the winter ice will soon be drinking up,

their rasped edges not like puzzle pieces
overlapping before they spiral away

and finally get caught up against the bank
where a kid might pick one up, let it

dry pressed in a book it'll fall out of
years later, reminder of an easiness

he once believed real: beneath a maple
before it's turned from green to red, tossing

seeds to watch them helicopter down
across a sky so blue it might break

his heart to remember on nights like this,
horizon smeared the color of fading coals.

Morning Begins with Dark

thunderstorms forming, kids out of school
        and off to camp, brand new ringtones
                loaded on phones. Another famous

overdose, another fading star
        on trial, a governor-gone-wild
                all sexier stories than missiles

on the move, protesters bleeding in streets
        of cities we struggle to find
                on maps, factories and their towns

shut down. Round-the-clock coverage spinning
        but every morning begins with dark,
                summer never a surprise. Again

the tide reaches shore, releases power
        it's held for miles, length and amplitude
                in a constant longing for land, sure,

but also the strong swimmer overcome
        by currents, by heat and half a case
                of beer, ripped out to sea and no one sees;

the moon and stars, nebulae giving
        birth, galaxies trailing to endless black
                at their edges, yes, but also

streetlamp haloes, one-way side streets spoked
        from city centers, cigarettes in
                shadows, smashed glass gritting underfoot.

From far enough away, I too become
        part of a sun, even my darkness
                only part of a star burning up,

the order of the universe enough
        to make me want, awake at night, to cry.
                Tiptoe through meadows, treading not to crush

a butterfly pollinating lupine,
        or squash them all to save Topeka?
                Some moments, any place feels like home:

buckeyes drumming California hillsides, hail
        on a prairie, cottonwood fleecing
                a canyon floor, snow in Boston streets.

Semblance, similitude, synchronicity:
        everything comes together until what
                happens is nothing special, nothing new.

Comets, glaciers, extinctions, histories
        happened, happen, over and over,
                and we're doomed, not because we never learn

but just because we are. Everyone knows
        empires rose to collapse, but we're slow,
                so slow, to see what comes our way,

each fall like the first, each loss, shocked
    that the locusts are back, the wheat
        eaten beyond what we can suffer.

Skies Clearing

(Portola Valley, CA)

Fog burning off gives way
            to stretches of blue

unadorned: an idea
            of infinity startles

and fades, a dropped pebble
            in a pond, ripples, nothing—

how it feels that first time
            you make blood trickle

from a quivering lip, each
            drop blotting the cirrus

white of skin, spotting
            his cotton tee, a stain

which unlike innocence
            pales but never completely

goes away. On another coast
            another time, sunlight

piled above the tide
            color by color, crowding

out the night, unmistakable
            as a type of faith,

but waking up here
		it's nearly impossible

to imagine the clouds
		passing—like believing

I walk in these woods
		alone, the dead not watching

my path, like admitting
		the earth cracks apart

right here beneath my feet—
		until they do, and fog

becomes an essay
		on gravity and fate

whose claims won't hold up
		in morning's breaking light.

Like Dreams, Seasons Passing

My fingers numb on the keys, crowd
watching my hands skip along
a ledge of hymn. I didn't want

to wake, not if chords kept coming,
so I played, crowd vanished, the ridge
a corpse stretched all the miles

to dawn. On a branch's lattice
of shadow I drummed, each hand
too slow, unable to follow the beat

of California buckeyes striking
yellow leaves. I needed to learn
it all, knew what silence I'd wake to.

Next morning, the woman I love
reached for my hand as we hiked
a ravine in the rain. We watched

banana slugs feel their way
along, crawling like suns, lifetimes
passing. We wondered where they go

when it's dry. We counted, bodies
bright on rotting ground, the rain
on redwoods a song overhead.

On the Twelfth Day of Christmas

(in Death Valley, 2008)

Walking on miles of salt
      so far below sea, I drown
            in its scent, ripples

rising as untimely heat.
      Two fighter jets returning
            to China Lake knife

the silence above, outrun
      the sound of themselves the way
            what's happening escapes

what language we have.
      Tomorrow we'll find out
            about another roadside

bomb and learn the names of more
      Marines killed—winter's
            symbolic grip on the year

just begun, the desert's
      undeserved reputation
            for lifelessness. I climb out

of heat, and Joshua trees
      lift their limbs, their leaves
            daggers brandished at clouds

that scud past jagged peaks,
      each of them set aflame
            by the plummeting sun.

*****

Ice on a Dirt Road

doesn't glisten exactly, doesn't glint or flash
    but pulls you in regardless, pulls you in
        as you feel it start to spin you out

and toward the bank—water below
    so slow, sluggish river rolling over
        bouldered bottom, so slow you know

it's almost frozen, know how fast it would
    seep into bones, hold you under as skin
        turns numb, the rush of ripple and wave

unreal, unable to feel so you wouldn't
    believe the sound—till your heart
        in your ears beats and you remember

the wheel; rain falls faster, freezing
    as it hits, and the river creeps below
        even as its surface slows, stops, heat

of a heart coursing along, invisible
    arterial heat dissipated but not
        disappeared; then clouds, emptied, begin

to break and temperatures again threaten
    to drop, the road ready to do its worst:
        to remain a road once you've passed.

In the Months after His Death You Move through Moments Like a Mountain

waiting in the wind and wishing for mist to gather you in, gravity and weather to work together to keep you in place, the weight of water to contain you, hold you to yourself, for fog to rob you of vision and make you invisible. Instead the rains wash you over, erosion grinding you down, snowfields and glaciers erased to reveal the damage they've done over time. Time flies but not when you're a mountain, whole climates changing around you, ice sheets flowing and receding, bridges bringing peoples who eventually sow seeds of civilizations and raise stone temples, cities razed when empires fall, when crops fail or conquerors come or gods grow bored or all of the above at once, one word at a time languages losing their tongues and languishing, and you standing above it all, silent all the while, not quite as tall perhaps or flatter in spots, rock concealed or revealed by plants growing, by snow and ice, landslide, by wind, by fire. Time so rife with annihilation, so filled with ways to be worn down, no wonder you lean alone against storms, peek over clouds while stars spin their fleeting beacons in the infinite dark, surround yourself with valleys to catch and hold every piece that falls from your heights, every drop that runs down your sides.

Of the Pine-trees Crusted with Snow

When snow starts falling, falling at first
like cherry blossoms in warm wind, the tree
seems to lift like wings its branches, hover
    the way a lover lingered in a door
    and longing took hold before she was gone,

but then it happens so fast, the gathering
of this season and its distances,
you fail to notice the moment they sag,
    each limb like an arm held out to steady
    yourself as you stood to go after her.

And Mourners To and Fro Kept Treading

Halfway home and the sun collapses
        into the road ahead, every curve
threatening to wrench away the wheel.
        Don't go, the grass behind a guardrail

calls, nowhere to be but here, so hide
        from headlights always in close pursuit.
There is no home to return to, home
        the lie layered day by day until

there's no way of digging deep enough
        to extract what it is that fastens
me, to say what chains any of us
        to a place we forever circle

like a drain, a hole where once a star
        shone, once turned like a god looking back
to drag us along the path we have
        no hope of retracing in the dark.

I Grieve That Grief Can Teach Me Nothing

Road stippled with rain, I slam imaginary
brakes in the back seat. Sparrows in bushes

and I'm breathless, scanning for bear, cougar—
something to explain the brain's involuntary

circling the drain, a hole I can't fathom.
I'm sick and tired of dying—tired of its grip

on the belly's pit, sick of the shiver
it slips between beats, the ceiling's spin

before the heart settles back to its rhythm
and muscles unclench. In bed I used to pray

for everyone to make it through the night.
Now I lie awake and wait for day to break.

Say something, I beg the dead, tell me
it's easier in the moment to let it go

but they have no promise to give, and the list
of names grows daily longer until I know

to live is to gather dying about myself
like a quilt in the night, like sheets, like skin.

In April

In April the potholes could swallow you whole.

Pollen squalls across roads and falls on crews that patch them up, flashing lights and orange cones as sure a sign of spring as blowing off work for opening day.

In April pitchers blow in their hands and players leave trails of rising breath as they hustle base to base.

In April you run through rain and wait for May.

Playgrounds swarm with children sprung from apartments, fences lined with smiling moms and dads.

In April the asphalt's cracked and storms that pound the shoreline take away the shapes you know, undertow a grief you trust will sweep you off your feet without a word.

You tell yourself it won't be worse in April. It is. Worse: there's no explaining why. You lie and say it's the weather. Whether or not it rains the ground is wet.

In March the soil starts to thaw. By April soil's soft enough for seeds.

The earth is soft enough for sleep, deep enough to swallow you whole.

Record Flooding as Metaphor for Grief

Not the river rushing its banks and breaking

dams, overrunning sandbags stacked in the hours

before it crested. Not the unmeasured depth

that wrecks a pickup and the tow truck grinding

to haul it out, the mud-brown wall that splinters

trunks like twigs and rips up others, roots and all.

Not the risen water, not the raging waves,

but the basement slowly gaining back its shape:

seven feet of muck pumped out, a foundation

unhoused, four stone walls with only space to hold,

the contents of boxes spilled and spoiled—photos

and baby clothes soaking in sludge—all of it

exposed, opened up to sky, the sudden sky

and its cruel light pouring through what used to be

shelter, and nothing left to fill such a hole.

*****

Almanac

April sets us on the scent of summer, opens up a trail

but it's covered in mud. Buds on the branches but also mold

begins to stain the plaster walls. Patter of rainfall lulls me,

pulls me under after a week awake, weightless as I watch

the minutes flicker. We long for what comes next but never learn,

never learn to hold a moment in its wholeness, show our hand

at the table and take what comes, to know it comes regardless

so there's hardly sense in hoping for an outcome we can live

with—unchecked wealth and recession, infinite stars expanding

to collapse, matter folding inward to absorb all light as

focused mass, a blossom that opened hours before it wilts

under frost, love and its loss. We long for each season as if

its being brings finale. We barter our lions for lambs,

empty limbs for leaves and blooms, but soon discover the pollen

slipped into the package and there's no way of giving it back.

Spring Cleanup

Kicked to the curb, picked and pruned, refused
        and packed in paper bags—last year's leftover
leaves, creeper and prickers, pieces of rock

        a season of frost heaved through sandy soil, all
the bits of nature's bounty we cast aside
        to be carted off and turned to who-knows-what:

feed, fertilizer, decorative wreaths, smoke.
        We open the gates and wield our rakes
and clippers, stake a claim to nature's spillage.

        Our tillage may be futile in a week
but now: neat rows and fresh-trimmed limbs—blistered
        thumbs and thorn-sticks simple sacrifices

for a short-lived reprieve from the constant
        advance of crabgrass. Down the block, rows of bags
beside the road an honor guard: the over-

        abundance we've discarded sends us off,
the hardware store another stop on our way
        to a destination we pretend not to know.

April Fools

Big fat snowflakes spinning
                in wind, telephone wires whip

as if unwilling
        to hoist another load, to hold

the weight of winter any longer—
              easy to lay perspective on

the inanimate, animate
          the neighborhood's connective tissue

with my not quite rage
          but more than mild annoyance

that in like a lion out like a lamb is
              a bunch of horseshit.

Day by day this in and out
          just breaks me down,

the starting and stopping,
         not a trickle toward but a rush and recede

and the unfulfilled wish:
         that snow's the joke, calendar

flipped and the page ripped up and tossed
                                   to filter down,

to ticker-tape this constant slog
                        toward something better down the road.

Sonnet about Trees, Sort Of

From my window, buds above the sidewalk offer
again unrest. Yellow-weighted branches bleed
on neighbors' cars, windshields pollen-dusted, clumps
of it streaked across each driver's field of vision.

See: I still don't know what beauty is, can't pluck
its note from the mix. I sit and watch, wait for buds
to blossom, leaves to set themselves in place, transfixed
by the grip such delicate design can hold

for a time, transfixed to know six months from now
they'll stuff brown bags, feed backyard flames, clog gutters
to make puddles that freeze when frost touches down.

A bird settles on the sill and seems to look in
when it pecks the screen. I don't know what's worse: wanting
to say hello, or saying nothing at all.

Lines Written in Early Spring

Sixty-five and sunny, buds
      opened and limbs revising
            distant hills, music floods

the street from porches. Neighbors
      lean on brooms and rakes, listen
            to baseball, laughter almost

drowning out the fountain
      spray of pumps that spout
            from cellars, living room sets

laid out on lawns to fend off
      stench and staunch mold's spread.
            Like the calendar flips

and we forget, the breeze
      bangs screen doors and we sit
            on the stairs, beer in hand:

uncaged and chasing
      a scent of summer, racing
            as if they know already

everything is short-lived,
      kids run for how it feels
            to run, running and shouting

without words, without wasting
        breath on sensefulness—sense
                hard to make of sunlight

pulling petals from mud, sense
        a stranger to this season
                always about to retreat.

Complaint in Springtime

Maybe winter's not so bad:
        snowdrifts and sorrow mismatched
in measure, spring so brutal

        in its budding—floodwaters
mucking gutters and potholes
        torn open, traffic backed up,

rivers crested and roads
        closed. So much reminds me
what's gone, weeds choking

        roses, unflowering trees
bound in noxious creeper
        and how to get rid of it:

the rusted rake, the spade
        shoved down with a stomping
foot—hack the earth and strip

        its shell, fabric rent and rot
below exposed. Hands cracked
        and blistered, stuck with thorns

without a saint to take them
        out, I wish again for
winter, inches of snow

over sidewalks, lamppost
glow and the twilit oaks
like a host of sisters

and brothers open-armed:
bodies to rest against,
limbs unbroken, unbent.

April: Beside Lucy Brook

The parking lot dusty like summer
    but wildflowers sprouting from mounds

of gravel left behind when snowmelt
    runneled downhill and into the woods,

we climb for half a mile, autumn's
    leaves still soggy underfoot, to see

the rush, the rowdy meeting of rock
    and mountain runoff, water's constant

funneling down, chiseling its path
    through layer on layer, every splash

not quite an echo, cascades skimming
    over striations in stone the way

a voice fits itself to a story
    it's suddenly time to tell. Above

the falls, a massive slab of ice hangs
    from the mossy granite, dangles down

and drips itself into the brook, its
    trickle a whisper lost in the roar.

The Insomniac at the Full Moon

The moon can go screw,
   always poking through
the blinds, shifting
   its face nightly, hiding

a smirk in its waning
   shape, so full of
its crescent self,
   crepuscular shell

of day demanding
   center-stage and me
tucked in tight, hard-pressed
   by the weight

of its light.
   Orion can bite me, arrogant
prick, sickening in his
   single-mindedness:

sidereal reeling
   doesn't deter him
from his fruitless trek,
   simple-minded

in pursuit of lunar
   shadows that shape
my longest nights. Fuck
   that tow truck backing

into place, sirens on
        the parkway, freight trains
on the breeze. Sheep
        need counting and one's still

missing, slipped away
        and bleating, out
of reach and bleating
        for day to break.

*****

It Doesn't Show Signs of Stopping

If morning arrives as expected
      I'll shovel snow, make a path

for neighborhood kids to shuffle down
      to the park, their plastic sleds

in tow, every trail of breath that lifts
      behind them reminding me

we're always leaving, already gone
      when we get here, the way snow

starts to melt the moment it touches
      ground, the way a storm hits shore.

For now, the kids across the street press
      their faces to fogged glass, wait

for wheeling clouds to drop the first flake.
      They're only crossing fingers

for no school, but it won't be long till
      they watch like me—sick and tired

of season drifting into season
      under cover of darkness,

so tonight I'm trying not to fall
      asleep under pregnant skies

imagining how the end will come:
        the world we've always known hushed

by oblivion's slow sifting down;
        the newness of old objects

drifted to forms; blinding cold, white light.
        Tomorrow, snowplows grinding

to push back in place familiar shapes,
        I'll pull on boots and mittens

to do the same, lifting and pitching
        until I scrape to surface:

cracked and frost-heaved concrete, plastic jug
        flattened in the gutter, tuft

of yellowed crabgrass, crumb of frozen
        soil, soggy leftover leaf.

Yes, when morning comes I'll shovel
        and make a path, but for now,

tonight, right this moment, nothing falls
        through the haloes of lampposts

humming up and down the empty street
        and even the everynight

sirens are silent. A held breath hangs
        in city-light haze, as if

we're waiting for something (we always
        are) already on its way.

Everything Comes, It Seems, Like This

Sudden patter, steady tapping overhead—
    I expect acorns, birds and squirrels, not rain, not
the ground speckled, drop after drop alighting
    like a murder of crows on a summer field.

Thunder splinters, rattles, fades. The wind shivers
    unclad oaks, ripples summits of yellow grass
disappearing, daylight sunk behind the ridge.
    Night stretches longer with every setting sun.

Everything comes, it seems, like this: already
    dark, another season descended so soon.
Everything falls in the end but I hardly
    feel the rain. Once you're wet you can't get wetter.

When my father died I couldn't get enough
    of rain, its sound, this pitter, everything else
still. Down the valley, thunder cracks. I listen
    in rain's unmeasured rhythm for what comes next.

To My Child Before She Arrives

There is a man you will learn
        to call uncle. He will teach you
the answer to many questions

        is *land bridge.* There will be truth
in what he says. He will call you
        something other than your name

no matter what your name is.
        No matter what your name is
you might not like it. It is likely

        you will have lots of hair,
likely in places you would not
        expect. I have always tried

to play up my love
        for bears so even body fat seems
tribute to mothers who kill

        to protect their young. I hope
I would do the same. Let us
        see what happens. Whatever happens,

most of us feel we were born
        too late but really there are
no good old days. Some days

there will be only swallowed silence
and sobbing: the world is
            not always kind and rarely makes sense

so when the sun goes down
            we will sing our songs and talk
about morning. Mountain ranges

            rise from valleys and forests
make them look green, but mountains are
            mostly gray underneath, stone

we will sometimes climb simply
            to stand on top of. Sometimes
at sunset it looks like mountain

            and cloud are the same. When it does
please sit with me and watch.
            Lakes are best for swimming

and rivers for fishing but oceans
            wash away feelings you cannot find
names for. No matter what,

            drying your feet of cold water
will make them feel better
            than you can imagine,

especially after a day spent
            walking uneven ground. Reaching
the end of days, it is common

to ask, "Why are we here? Where
are we going? How do we get there?"
        There are lots of answers.

You will have to find most of them
        yourself. It will involve lots
of walking on uneven ground.

        It might involve trying
to walk across water. You could do
        worse than wet feet. There will be

sobbing and silence, unkindness,
        love, and laughter. You could do
lots worse. You could do lots. Do lots.

Winter's Come and Gone

To stand beside a river   and believe in rivers

is a wish for form, its hold   on what we see. Elsewhere

you imagine a river,   dream one into being

but here you lie in weeds   and wait for water to rise

and rise, raise your bones   and carry them off, for summer

to return, river without   snowmelt churning, eddies

empty, granite risen   from water as if come home.

After Hearing Cinderella's 1988 Hit "Don't Know What You Got (Till It's Gone)" I Wait by the Window

Any minute winter will break
      again, the way each day begins:
sun revises shadow, clouds
      revise the sky, and rains revise
the roadside dust from Boston
      to Chicago, where once I found
myself, tire-flapped trucks lifting
      mist, tempted to backtrack
and find the first drop, the instant
      blacktop went dry to wet, when
East became Midwest, but twilight
      had arrived. Another time
hesitant, knees buckled, rope
      burned fingers and I swung free
from the tree, watched water rush so
      clean but failed to see the moment
rise became fall. Every song
      fades into the next. Passing
minutes begin to unravel
      now a season I cannot name,

each word I have a wintered
    breath that vanishes even
before I hear who speaks.

To My Daughter Who Struggles to Sleep through the Night

Lost without my shoulder
       soaked in snot, rocking
your body to bed
       the way I know my day's
done, I'm waiting instead
       for day to break. Stars
spin through a window
       opened on crickets
not answering your hour
       by hour cries. Some nights
it's easy to believe
       a parent could shake
the baby, but the way
       this day won't end
without your weight
       in my arms, your legs
pinned against my hip,
       makes me aware
of you in futures I
       won't witness, aware
your life and mine
       make sense in coming
together each night
       beside your crib, floorboards
creaking underfoot
       as your voice relaxes
to match my own, hush
       and whisper and breath, heavy

breath of sleep when
        you've fallen at last
asleep and stay
        asleep, when I realize
you're asleep and it's safe
        to put you down and leave you
until morning alone.

One to Another

Wind whispers no secrets. It rips and roars, steals
what's said and carries it down ridges

to the valley. You catch a glint of ocean
eighty miles away, but listen: not waves, no tide

doing its constant dance. The wind carving
granite takes and gives nothing back. Watch:

hats flipping over their brims, tattered maps
snagged on scrub pine curling into itself

as clouds part just enough for sun to edge aside
the chill, warm enough on wind-whipped faces

for smiles, for favors. If the camera pilfers
bits of soul, then what does the eye behind it

take, what binds the hiker who snapped your photo
and the campers who posed as you counted?

Camaraderie and camera: vaulted room
and roommate: strangers made companions

under a vault of clouds. It doesn't happen
at malls, in parks, on buses. Beaches, it's keep

to your blanket. But up here something scatters
the self, the way blueberries cram every crack

holding water from storm to storm, the way
clouds gather around the summit, birds

to a spire, the way—like this—simile
finds simile, one to another, language

piling up and meaning diffused till it comes
together, likeness accreting the way

stone on stone becomes a mountain that stands
alone against wind coming out of the north.

Blue Hills, Early December

Rusted chain-link rising from tall grass, mud
    crunching underfoot, the bluster dying down

divulging the rush of highway from below—this is no mountain,
    that no valley. But still something up here's

required, requires uncontracted time to cast about,
    feet unattached from the path, to wander

windswept granite, cores exposed,
    hilltops weather-undressed, time to watch, to rest:

contact, confluence of stone and flesh, matching contours
    of bedrock and backside, the body's

ability to shape itself, shift its limits and puzzle-piece
    with the ground, ground itself, be grounded

against solid rock, bedrock found, foundation felt
    as principle of living on this earth where what we get

is hardly the world we expect, every
    earthly encounter not exactly what we wish for.

So low it gives small warmth the sun
        shines back from the skyline, coppers the wrinkled

harbor. Flights sliding out of Logan silent from here,
        every contrail a cloud that fails to fill the sky

and so dissolves the way this season slips away—
        sugar maple with its last flags, puritan brown

of oak rooted to this landscape in ways we can't
        recall, comprehend, reclaim. But still longing lingers:

to settle, set the feet deep in the duff, sink
        through dirt down to bedrock, the hard bottom, to be

as seasons spirit themselves around me, assume
        my every atom, some transition, transformation,

some threshold trying to slip itself past, catch me
        unaware, unready, resting my eyes, taking a breath.

There's snow on the way, its offer of erasure,
        oblivion, newness in nothingness, utter unfamiliarity,

more inviting than resurrection blossoms of spring, rebirth
        overrated, the regular repetition of it, unthinking

reiteration, reification of past actions, accentuation of what came
        before and comes again and again, again and again.

What we get is almost always the willow, always
        the cherry blossom, tulips splitting soil in the same

furrowed space, each spring a palimpsest
        of every other, hardly ever what we wish for:

the bare branch,
        blank page, unwritten word, unturned earth.

✶✶✶✶✶

Watson and the Shark

after John Singleton Copley

From the leather bench, legs swinging
    a foot from the floor, she brings her gaze
to the shark: its hideous teeth, its misplaced
    lips and mistaken shapes, the sinister
        way its mass slips beneath the surface

to surface again as a scythe-shaped fin.
    I follow strokes of light converging
on the crew, every body strained to save the naked boy
    but one, his face hauntingly matter-of-fact,
        the pact a sailor makes with the sea

a tacit acceptance of death in all
    its disgraceful forms. If she sees
what I'm seeing, she's not saying.
    Now she paces, takes in details to piece
        together, then climbs back onto the bench

and clambers off again. She stops and stares:
    bloodied leg, sailors' hands outstretched, Watson
reaching out toward something past the boat,
    past clippers, slave ships, masts like crosses
        and holy towers on shore, past

the horizon and its amassing
    clouds, where waves vanish in the rising sun
the shark has come from and will return to
    after playing with the man who's falling
        asleep in the water. "Isn't it silly?"

she asks as she turns away from the canvas
        and smiles up at a man who's stopped
to look and listen to headphones explaining
        Copley's shift from portraits to works
                of historical ambition, myth made

from the everyday, and she tells him
        the boo-boo's not so bad, they'll get him
in the boat and take good care of his leg.
        The stranger nods—not quite sure, I'm sure,
                of what's taking place but maybe

grateful everything will be okay—
        and walks away as my daughter settles
on the bench and waits: for the painting
        to change, for the sun to rise, for me
                to take her hand and let her lead me on.

Solstice

In Boston today the trains wait

    on tracks. Trucks push piles of snow

up piles of snow. No one's getting in

    or going out. Hours of coffee

and cable news, a folding table

    forms the space a jigsaw puzzle

frames and fills, the picture taking

    shape as every figure outside's

slowly rounded, mounded under

    a daylong fade to white.

I wait for night to come without

    its dark, for flakes to taper off

and clouds to pull apart, for stars

    and the day's accumulated

falling to reflect their light, luster

    offered up by streets I knew

till now, each house a ghost against

    the sky. I hold my breath. Tonight

I will not shut my eyes.

In Summer the Song Sings Itself

We must tease it out from every surface in winter,
must shovel-scrape asphalt, push the blizzard-drift
aside, slide, scuff, lift and flip, must free up space for feet, breath
rising in huffs and puffs the flakes keep falling through, piling
faster than thoughts of the infinite flee our feeble grasp,
the before and after this-the-only-life-we-know impossible
to conceive, the mind-at-work freezing even as flesh
heats itself on quickened pulse, pounding heartbeat—
and here we get back to the sidewalk-search for song, somehow
gone astray and the song still far off, so we must focus back
on snowfall through breath, shovel tip scraping, scratching
lawn-edge, letting loose leaf-rot and flash of green, grime
of mud, sterile field of winter smudged, suddenly death
or life or something in between appearing, another season
showing itself too soon, the earth not nearly far enough along
to grant another spring its start, another grace its birth,
but there it is, a glimpse of what we're hardly aware
we're looking for, trying to tease out, get to the bottom of, so
we must look, longing, lick it maybe, lap it up, plunge
down, dig bottomlessly, split the frigid ground and hope
to hit bedrock, bust it open, break it in pieces and bring it up
by bucketloads, big break-in, making our own way, earth
opened up and admitting us into a womb where summer
and the song that sings itself exist untouched by this cold,
until all of it, warmth and the song we seek, works
its way back up to the surface and sprinkles decay
among the snow, decay and life, life and decay really two sides
of the same one-way street, fertile soil piling up now,

mittened hands hard at work, shovel tossed aside, then
our mittenless hands ripping up snow and soil and song
by fistfuls, fitful effort to grasp what we find before getting
back to what we haven't and suspect we must keep searching for.

Three-Year-Old Makes the Visiting Poet's Portrait

From the back of the hall, his voice a call to song,
        to singing, bringing to music whatever past we have.
                She slips from my lap when his voice passes along

something for her alone to claim, and she starts
        reshaping him, lines unsteady but pressed deep,
                reality what she knows best: the purity

of crayon to paper, prime colors the measure
        she makes of everyone, simple shapes. She tears it
                from her pad and runs to him, offers it up

for his fridge. He lays it down beside his books—mismatched
        stick-figure arms reaching out, mouth opened wide
                and the blue of his shirt the brightest in the box.

Watch the River Flow

        I lived once where the river turns north
as if it could return to its source, climb
        the latitudes back through time and pass
the meeting of Pemigewasset
        and Winnipesaukee, come
to the cliff where the Old Man lies
        in heaps of granite, gravity
having won again. It always does
        but still I'm caught off guard, a child
who stacks whatever he finds, block
        on block, pebbles and rocks, the topple
always a shock. I'd walk in spring
        and watch its cresting water fall
over dams and locks, its constant
        drilling into bedrock, downhill
run to continent's edge. I'd stop
        to study the spot where it turns
and tries to revise the maps but only
        winds up flowing east to lose itself
in seas, snow and rain diffused
        in the Gulf of Maine and hauled away
by currents and tides a mountain
        wouldn't imagine even if mountains

could, a summit's slow erosion
          nothing compared to an ocean's
pounding, the steady pull of a moon.

April: Beside Pawtucket Gatehouse

The river hits flood stage and falls
          crash louder than traffic, rocks
                    wrapped in mist or decked with debris

the rest of the year now visible
          only by eddies where they break
                    the current—a heart and its beating

proven by the pulse's steady pause.
          We measure its depth by watching
                    graffiti on the bridge go under.

Imagine the wreckage of roads
          washed away. Picture the wrack swept
                    over gates and locks, ruined bodies

surfaced and churning downstream.
          Grief might surge, immediate
                    nostalgia for all that passes,

until we notice: we touch for once
          what drowns us instead of knowing
                    we sink but not what drags us down.

The City I Come From Responds

And yet you return again, revisit this strip of brick on brick
because when every word's put down and you're put in a field,
casketed, covered with snow, this is where you come from: river
dammed and channeled, dammed and released, winter runoff
        flowing
eternally deeper through rocky earth where nothing much grows.
From every life a little grief, I know, but give it up, go on, grow up,
get over it: get a job, a hobby, get a horse. Holler yourself
hoarse at baseball, hockey, watch your neighbors' faces reflected
in ice, lights and sirens singing something like pride each time a
        puck's
jammed five-hole. Holy hell, jump from your seat. By their joy, by
        jubilation
know you've found a home, no home you knew now lingering
        here, no
longer the valley you left, valley filling with tumbled brick. Listen:
music moves nightly over water, music and laughter, the
        Merrimack's
noise, its never-ending nosedive over the falls, nearly silenced by
over-the-top applause, standing ovations and always one more
        encore,
performers pleased to return, eager to come and play for crowds
quite happy they stayed, content and not, like you, in constant
        quandary.
Remember strolling the river path, parents sharing a cone,
        remember
sandlot baseball, swelter of stone dust underfoot, then the rope
        swing

tossing you at the stagnant canal, its bottom cool between your
    toes.
Until you left you never uttered such unhappiness, hindsight's
vision of living within these limits too quick to revise
what good gets wrapped in history's warp and weft. By whatever
axis you map yourself, exile's exhausting. Whatever tracks
you followed out will lead you back. Year by year a river's
zealous rise and fall will raze and restore your only holy ground.

*****

Prayer for Something Like a Home

Let me learn to love
this land, the lay of
the highways, the maze
of crooked one-ways
cobbled together
in colonial
haste. Give me a place
to linger, to wait
for sirens to drown
in distance, for wind
to gust, its bluster
among the maples
almost mistaken
for a forest song.
If long winters claim
me, let me come from
cold and know myself
by slogging toward home
through snow. I will don
the proper smock, wear
a hairshirt molded
to my bones, worn soft
in all the right spots.
If landscape once was
sacramental, then
let me dig in mud
and dust, smear its mark
across my brow, wash
my feet in moving

waters when I step
into its river,
and let me never
find the other side.
Let me learn to name
this green, that purple,
chartreuse and lilac,
lavender. Let me
welcome ash-gray skies
as perfect background
for colors coming
out of nowhere, gift
we must let go of.

A Note to the Neighbor on the Corner

Mortality's bite is tough to chew for most of us—can you
imagine how much tougher for the kid who never sees
her grandfather & wants to know why her grandmother lives

alone in a house with so many beds & why your beds
of flowers never bloom like others up & down the block?
The porcelain goose & plastic flamingos don't help—

her consternation & concern for birds who never move
still raising weighty questions later as we swing & slide.
I hope everything's okay with you but I have to say:

broken bottles, empty jugs, the decapitated duckling
lying in weeds are starting conversations I'd planned
to wait a couple years at least to have. I'm not much

for miracles, not much for masking those realities
that make my nightly dread, but she has a lot of years left
to ponder death & I'd like for your house not to haunt her yet.

No Small Comfort

Branches bare on Friday
    managed to bud by Monday morning—

my weekend hike beside a creek
    to find a centuries-old grindstone

not nearly as impressive
    as winter-dormant blossoms

making their sudden yellow show
    against blue sky, my newest lines

about seasons spinning into place
    with storm after storm

no match for photosynthesis
    setting itself in motion again.

Every tree spreads its leaves
    and converts the atmosphere to food

using water and sunlight, feeding itself and
    releasing what I need

to breathe. Me?
    In a couple of weeks I can grow a beard

that catches crumbs
    from a toasted steak and cheese.

It's impossible, turning the corner
           to millions of these little flags

unfurling, not to be impressed
           by a world that makes itself over

each day. It baffles, befuddles
           to think of living, breathing

creatures seeming all but dead all winter
           one day flourishing

colors and textures and odors
           I hardly recognize after months

of shielding my eyes from the glare
           of snow and ice, turning away

from bare branches and the longing
           empty space between them makes.

In a mind made numb by winter
           it's easy to accept

doing the same thing over and over
           and hoping for different results

as a version of insanity. Really
           it's no small comfort to know

what grows before our eyes keeps going:
           trees coming into bloom

or two-day whiskers on my chin, or the skin
            on my hands scored by scars.

Under all there's
            little difference.

In a world that cuts us—
            every last one of us—down,

it's no small comfort to see
            what we see and be overcome.

For My Love

I too am easy like Sunday morning.
I've tried to begin a poem with that line
for years, even though it's simply not true—
at best I'm needy, tricky to live with,

moody like a two-year-old. At its worst
I know my sadness may become your grief.
But now, as morning seeps across the room,
leave your coffee cooling in its cup, walk

beside me to the top of Peters Hill
and watch the arboretum spread its limbs
below, the city asleep and the sun
too low for shadow. Please remember this

throughout the week, remember how at times
I too am easy like Sunday morning.

Thorndike Street

strangely never changes, not enough to feel forgot
        no matter how long I've stayed away, how prodigally
I've strayed. Off the Connector, exit wrapping around
        itself until the underpass opens up like time

turning back: I'd swear the same Matador's been sitting
        on the curb for thirty years, the factory outlet's
COMFORT FURNITURE a promise of the minimum
        home might still provide. Even Gallagher Terminal's

improvements make little difference—name a train station
        that doesn't look decades old and I'll buy your ticket
to any misremembered place you want to return.
        Heading downtown, shiny signage reads of renewal

but surely this takes love: the same potholes patched again
        and again, the street signs naming the constant path home.

Neighborhood Ode

Praise the bare branch, broken
       planters spilling soil and seeds unseen

till spring. Praise the icicle's daily
       melt and nightly freeze, reminder

every season gathers and scatters all
       at once, ever a harvest and ever

its chaff. Praise the chaff, make
       of it altars. Praise the wreckage

of every act, patches of yellow grass
       and mounds of shoveled snow, howling

wind and summer's stagnant heat. Praise
       the cello and the cellist who lugs it

on a crowded bus. Praise
       buses, praise trains, the driver

who rings a bell for a child
       who waves and waits for another

to pass her way. Praise the way
       of trolleys and trains, buses

rumbling round and round, a song
       the child sees and so believes in song.

Raven to a Traveler Lost in the Woods

After snap and splinter,
    after thunder

of trunk, shudder
    subsiding

till singular hush
    takes hold, hold

your breath. Listen for dust
    settling back

among grass, for sudden
    gap to fill again,

for errant leaves to flutter,
    to corkscrew down.

Even unfamiliar light
    hums, murmur

in ear that reaches
    deeper every second

breath inhabits your body's
    hollows. Follow

my shadow crossing,
    wings riffling

air around your head. Let me
      lead you in summer

song, long-rehearsed
      verse of praise

for ways space opens up
      a place once known,

for ways worlds remake
      themselves at every turn.

My Daughter Gathers Rocks Wherever She Goes

As if she knows erosion
to be the only constant. As if
she could reverse it, only time
and room to stack the limiting factors.

As if she could hold the whole
earth, the trick not finding the pieces
but fitting her fingers around them.

Pockets filled, digging in grass
for granite and quartz, rock after rock
stacked on the puddingstone poking
from hilltops glaciers left behind.

The way we trace a line
from star to star, as if a story
could order the chaos—infinite
expansion made to obey the laws
of coloring books—as if the stars
might never dim, never collapse.

Wherever she goes,
a singular searching, unshakable.

The way that generations
built their temples block by block, rock's
seeming permanence how we measure
ourselves to the day ahead: another
place to excavate, another stretch
of empty sky to fill up with our shapes.

*****

Evidence of Having Been Here

Someone's covered all this ground
        before. Retreating glaciers left
stones for travelers to stack

        and mark the path. I watch for them
wherever I walk, add a rock
        and prop up topples, build my own

beside a river. Winter's swell
        will carry some away, lay them
in alluvial fans downstream.

        *

Fossils, tools, weapons, every pot
carbon-dated. Observations,
equations, extrapolations.
Genomes mapped, invisible pasts
uncoded and available
online. Billion-dollar dishes
listen for proof something else is
out there. So much is conjecture,
an expert faith that will crumble
under cross-examination.
Once, the sun circled a flat earth.

        *

T-shirts, caps, cotton boxers tagged
        with initials. My father wore
coveralls to work with his name
        stitched across the breast pocket.

Week after week our hand-me-down
        washer pulled it apart: *Art*
unraveling thread by thread
        until an anonymous blue

stretched across his chest, only
        an empty pocket buttoned up.

                *

Newspaper yellows, clippings
crisp in scrap books. Initials
        carved in bark—trees grow

to fall and rot. A name traced
on frosted windowpanes—take
        a breath and it's gone.

Granite erodes, inscriptions
rubbed away and chiseled dates
        rounded off with time.

                *

What's framed once happened, if only
for one one-hundredth of a second:

six-year-old me about to spill
a plastic party cup, my brother

blowing, his candles still lit,
all of it light and shadow, glossed

paper. Moments fill shoeboxes, slip
between attic floorboards, corners

curled. I want the legends to be true:
let the camera take my soul, hold it

still, ever exposed to failing light.

*

What there is is here, is now:

baseball, laughter, houseboats (house

boats!) in San Francisco Bay,

cello, taste of skin. My breath

fogs, in morning light, the glass.

A train whistle always calls

the distance, a pair of crows

always scrawling a ballad

across the sky. There is time

to notice flowers bursting

from mud at a river's edge.

Acknowledgments

I am grateful to the editors of the following publications in which some of these poems first appeared, sometimes in slightly different form.

Barn Owl Review: "A Lake Opens Up Beneath Your Feet"

Breakwater Review: "Landscape with Primary Colors"

Cave Wall: "April: Beside Lucy Brook," "No Small Comfort"

Compose: "A Note to the Neighbor on the Corner," "Skies Clearing"

Conduit: "To My Daughter Who Struggles to Sleep through the Night"

The Cortland Review: "Neighborhood Ode"

The Cossack Review: "Everything Comes, It Seems, Like This"

Crab Creek Review: "I Grieve That Grief Can Teach Me Nothing," "On the Twelfth Day of Christmas"

DIAGRAM: "Blue Hills, Early December"

Flyway: Journal of Writing & Environment: "After Hearing Cinderella's 1988 Hit "Don't Know What You Got (Till It's Gone)" I Wait by the Window," "One to Another," "Watch the River Flow"

Four Way Review: "Almanac," "To My Child Before She Arrives"

The Georgia Review: "*Watson and the Shark*"

Grist: The Journal for Writers: "It Doesn't Show Signs of Stopping"

Gulf Stream: "The Insomniac at the Full Moon"

Hartskill Review: "April: Beside Pawtucket Gatehouse," "The Morning Air Is All Awash with Angels"

Luna Luna: "Of the Pine-trees Crusted with Snow"

Mid-American Review: "Record Flooding as Metaphor for Grief"

The Midnight Oil: "And Mourners To and Fro Kept Treading"

North American Review: "Thorndike Street"

The Pinch: "Complaint in Springtime," "Ice on a Dirt Road"

Poet Lore: "Lines Written in Early Spring"

Radar Poetry: "Late Night, Walking Home"

RHINO: "Raven to a Traveler Lost in the Woods," "Three-Year-Old Makes the Visiting Poet's Portrait"

River Mouth Review: "Evidence of Having Been Here"

The Rupture: "In the Months after His Death You Move through Moments Like a Mountain"

Salamander: "Morning Begins with Dark," "Prayer for Something Like a Home"

Sinking City: "In April"

Southern Humanities Review: "My Daughter Gathers Rocks Wherever She Goes"

Sugar House Review: "Winter's Come and Gone"

Third Coast: "The City I Come From Responds"

UCity Review: "Sonnet about Trees, Sort Of"

Valparaiso Poetry Review: "Spring Cleanup"

Vinyl Poetry: "Solstice"

Waccamaw: "In Summer the Song Sings Itself"

"The Morning Air Is All Awash with Angels" takes its title (and more) from "Love Calls Us to the Things of This World" by Richard Wilbur. "Of the Pine-trees Crusted with Snow" takes its title from "The Snow Man" by Wallace Stevens. "And Mourners To and Fro Kept Treading" takes its title from "I felt a Funeral, in my Brain" by Emily Dickinson. "I Grieve that Grief Can Teach Me Nothing" takes its title from "Experience" by Ralph Waldo Emerson. "It Doesn't Show Signs of Stopping" takes its title from "Let It Snow!" lyrics by Sammy Cahn. "Winter's Come and Gone" takes its title from "Winter's Come and Gone" by Gillian Welch and David Rawlings. "In Summer the Song Sings Itself" takes its title from "The Botticellian Trees" by William Carlos Williams. "Watch the River Flow" takes its title from "Watching the River Flow" by Bob Dylan. "For My Love" refers to the Commodores song "Easy," lyrics by Lionel Richie.

I am grateful for support from the Bread Loaf Writers' Conference and The Writer's Center.

Thank you to everyone at Black Lawrence Press, especially Diane Goettel.

Thank you to Keetje Kuipers and Matthew Olzmann, for their support and for their own astonishing poems.

Thank you to the many people whose inspiration, encouragement, and friendship carried me through the years it took to gather these poems, including Melanie Allen, Idris Anderson, William Archila, Mario Alejandro Ariza, Lory Bedikian, Jody Bolz, Jan Bottiglieri, Catherine Bull, Kai Carlson-Wee, Bryan Castille, Jessamine Chan, MRB Chelko, Abigail Cloud, Connie Congdon, Stephen Corey, Brittney Corrigan, Emily Carson Dashawetz, Jaquira Díaz, Nina Emery, Cai Emmons, John Findura, Jonterri Gadson, Miriam Gershow, Christine Gosnay, Elizabeth Harlan-Ferlo, Greg Hill, G. Grant Holtzberg, Garrett Hongo, Julia Halprin Jackson, Major Jackson, Lauren Kay Johnson, Chris Jones, Dorianne Laux, Melissa Lawlor, Keith Leonard, Sally Wen Mao, Paul Marion, Glyn Maxwell, Nathan McClain, Jill McDonough, Teo Mungaray, Mark Novom, Tom Nunan, Patrick Oh, Michelle Peñaloza, Susan Pogue, Joshua Robbins, Anthony Robinson, David Roderick, Brian Russell, Jeffrey Schultz, Solmaz Sharif, Tom Sleigh, Arthur Smith, Jess Smith, Sebastian Stockman, Tess Taylor, Kim Townsend, Brian Turner, Pimone Triplett, Keith S. Wilson, Arielle Zibrak, and especially Laura Passin and Kate Westhaver.

Thank you to the students and teachers who have learned alongside me over the years.

Thank you to Jason Vermillion, whose friendship reminds me who I am and who I want to be.

Thank you to my brother Scott, whose imagination nourished mine from the very start.

Thank you to my mother Karen, whose love still lights the long road home.

Thank you to Amelia, Harper, and Phoebe, for taking my hand and leading the way.

And thank you to Tregony, always, for walking beside me on every path.

In memory of Donald Pogue and Arthur Simoneau.

Brian Simoneau is the author of the poetry collection *River Bound*, which was selected for the 2013 De Novo Prize. Originally from Lowell, Massachusetts, he lives near Boston with his family.